Ruabon Boys Grammar School

RUABON
BOYS GRAMMAR SCHOOL

a collection of pictures

Dennis W. Gilpin

bridge
books

First published in Wales in 1999
by
BRIDGE BOOKS
61 Park Avenue
Wrexham
LL12 7AW

ISBN 1-872424-77-5

A CIP catalogue entry for this book is
available from the British Library

Printed and bound by
MFP, Stretford, Manchester

Introduction

This book is not intended to be a complete history of the Ruabon Grammar School. My main aim has been to highlight certain significant events that occurred at the school over the years and provide, whenever possible, glimpses of the lives of past students and staff by means of photographs and personal recollections. No story of the school would be complete without the inclusion of the Ruabon Girls Grammar School but, unfortunately, a lack of surviving photographs of that establishment has meant that it had to be excluded from this volume. Should any reader know of the whereabouts of any pictures, they might care to contact the publisher so that this omission can be rectified in the future.

For the early history of the school I am greatly indebted to articles written by Mr. A. H. Williams, MA (HMI) and the Rev. W. Pritchard (former Vicar of Ruabon and Archdeacon of Powys).

I should like to thank Derek Owens, the Old Boys' Association and its Secretary Gareth Davies, E. Tegwyn Williams, Ieuan Davies, Graham Pritchard, Franklin Roberts, Mary Saunders, Don and Glenys Jones, Edna Morris, Mary Rogers, Iola Hughes, Myra Edwards, Eva Parry, Kay Edwards, Dora Williams, Marian Prydderch, Gareth P. Hughes, Beverly Thomas, J Owain Jones, Paul Drake, Geoffrey Kilfoil, Llywelyn Williams, Gareth Thomas, Peter Davies, Glyn Hughes, Kinross Almond for providing all the photographs, programmes etc.. Thanks also to many others who have assisted in the naming of the individuals in the photographs and although there are a few omissions — hopefully few errors— I can assure you that every effort has been made to be correct and complete.

I should also like to acknowledge the contributions of John Smout in providing copies of the plans of the school and Christopher J Coyle for drawing up the final plan of the buildings.

The personal recollections of past pupils and staff form important and revealing parts of the book. I am deeply grateful to them for their invaluable contributions.

I am also very grateful to Gareth P. Hughes, an old pupil and Welsh master at the school for a number of years, who volunteered for the unenviable task of proof reading this book and for his encouragement during its preparation. Lastly, I thank my wife Elisabeth for all her assistance during the past months.

Dennis W. Gilpin
1999

An Outline History of the
Ruabon Boys Grammar School

In the early hours of the morning of Saturday March 5th, 1858 a fire broke out at Wynnstay, Ruabon, the home of Sir Watkin Williams Wynn Bt.. Fanned by a gale force wind, the fire swept quickly through the building and left it completely gutted in a matter of hours. Fortunately there were no casualties but thousands of pounds worth of furniture, paintings, jewellery, clothes and other treasures were destroyed.

However, probably the greatest tragedy was the loss of irreplaceable original Welsh manuscripts and the records of Ruabon Boys Grammar School, which covered the whole history of the school since its foundation. A chaplain at Wynnstay was researching the history of the parish of Ruabon and had borrowed the school records from the then headmaster, the Rev. A. L.Taylor. These were located in the library near to where the fire started. The parish records of Ruabon would have suffered the same fate had not the vicar of Ruabon, the Rev. R. Bonner Maurice, insisted that they should be returned to Ruabon Church each evening before dusk.

The destruction of these records has made the compilation of the history of the school extremely difficult. A few dedicated historians have however succeeded in uncovering sufficient information to trace some of the early history.

Thomas Ednyfed (Nevitt), the earliest benefactor.

In his article on 'The Origins of the Old Grammar Schools of Denbighshire' A. H. Williams has given a detailed description of the early history of the school. He quotes the Report of the Assistant Charity Commissioner for 1837 which states that a certain Thomas Nevitt (or Nevett), citizen and draper of London and a member of the Girdlers' Company, left a legacy of £2 a year to the schoolmaster at Ruabon in 1633. This statement can be accepted without question for it is corroberated by the copy of Nevitt's will at Somerset House.

In the will, Thomas Nevitt instructed that a tenement and twenty four acres of fresh marsh land in Romney Marsh should be bought by the Girdlers' Company and that they in turn should: "… truly pay or cause to be paid the somme of three pounds and fifteen shillings of lawfull money of England in manner and forme following (that is to say) To the Schoolemaster of the new erected free Schoole in Ruabon in the countie of Denbigh aforesaid for his better maintenance for teaching of poore men's children there the yearely somme of fforty shillings to be paid unto him on the first daye of November in every yeare yearely — and if it happen the said schoole shal be discontynued and there shal be noe schoolemaster there to teach and instruct children then my will and mind is that the said Master and Wardens of the said Art or Mistery of the Girdlers of London from tyme to tyme for the tyme being shall well and truly pay or cause to be paid the said yearely somme of forty shillings (soe lymited to be by them paid to the said schoolemaster as aforesaid) unto forty poore persons of the said parish of Ruabon such as the Parson or Minister and church wardens and others of the moste grave and discreeted parisheners of the same parish shall make choice of to be equally distributed amoungst them on St. Thomas day yearely."

In the will he also left 10s. to the vicar of Ruabon for preaching a sermon every Good Friday and 20s. to be distributed by him immediately afterwards amoung 30 deserving poor people.

It can be deduced from Thomas Ednyfed's will that he had accumulated a vast amount of wealth and that he wished that some of it be used to the benefit of his native countrymen. The sermon mentioned in the will was preached in Welsh for a number of years at Ruabon church.

The name Ednyfed appears frequently in the parish registers of Ruabon and Nevitt is the anglicized form of the name. For many years, in the absence of any other evidence, this document resulted in the year 1632 being generally accepted as the year of the foundation of the school. There is little doubt that Thomas Ednyfed was the school's earliest benefactor.

The Petition of 1637

The Rev. T. W. Pritchard, former vicar of Ruabon and archdeacon of Powys, has carried out very detailed research into the history of the school and in his article 'A History of the Old Endowed Grammar School, Ruabon, 1618–1896' reveals new evidence from which it is now possible to conclude that the school was actually founded in 1618. The evidence lies amoungst the Carreglwyd collection of documents at the National Library of Wales in the form of a letter or petition dated 9th June, 1637 and is addressed to "William Doctor att Lawes and Chauncellor of St. Asaphe and Bangor". It reads as follows:

Right wor'll,

May it please you to bee advertized That whereas there is a decent Schoolehouse errected uppon the North-syde of the Church-yard of the pishe of Ruabon within the Countie of Denbigh and dioces of St.Asaphe about these xlxth yeares agoe now last past by the generall consent of Mr.Doctor Lloyd Vicar of Ruabon and the gentlemen, ffreeholders and Inhabitants of the said pishe, & uppon their Comon Chardges, for the educateinge and instructinge of the Youthes of the said pishe and others with Learninge in the feare of God; And whereas som. doe feare least that hereafter the said Schoole-house might bee misymployed & converted to be an Alehouse or otherwise to a worse use then it was first intended. WE therefore the p'sons whose names are here subscribed beinge ffreehoulders and Inhabitants within the said pishe of Ruabon doe hereby humbly intreat yor.worp. That you would bee pleased to confirme the same School house to the use yt was first intended by due course of Lawe, And in the meane time to grant us yor. worps. Ires of Proclamation to cite all manner of p'sons that have any right or title to the said Schoolhouse or to the place where uppon the sane is erected to app'e with all convenyent speede before yor worp. uppon some Court Day at St. Asaphe to shewe cause why the said Schoole house should not bee by yor. worp. for ever confirmed to that good use whereunto it was first intended; In soe doeinge wee shall bee much obliged to pray for yor. worps. health. And so wee take Leave and remayne

Ruabon the x1x of	Yor. worps. assuredly in any	
June	Service wee may	
1637	Richard Lloyd vicar	
Roger Kinaston		
Wardens	John Lloyd	Tho. Evanse
John Peck	Jer. Davies Schoolmst.	
Edward ap Rondell	Eyton Evanse.	

It can be deduced from the petition that the school was supported by the people of the parish of Ruabon and provided free education for the children of that parish with provision for other children outside its boundaries.

There is little doubt that Dr. Richard Lloyd, father of Humphrey Lloyd (bishop of Bangor, 1673-1688), founded the school in 1618 soon after his arrival at Ruabon. The period following the Reformation enabled people to become aware of the importance of education in their advancement both economically and politically. The establishment of the school was thus of great importance to the inhabitants of Ruabon parish.

The Rev. Jeremiah Davies, A.M. was the first schoolmaster appointed at the school. His Letters of Orders, dated 1626, are to be found amoungst the Wynnstay manuscripts at The National Library of Wales. He began his work in 1626 and remained there until 1637 when he was succeeded by the Rev. Edward Pritchard, B.A., M.A. who was schoolmaster until 1668 and who also endowed the school. In all probability the school continued until the time of the Rev. John Robinson, B.A. who became schoolmaster in 1675, even though the Civil War had made it difficult to transmit money from the bequest of Thomas Ednyfed. Details about the numbers of children at the school and the curriculum followed during the 17th. Century have yet to be found.

The Rev. John Robinson was at Ruabon for 31 years and he first endowed the school in 1703 when he bequeathed Cinders Farm in the parishes of Ruabon and Bangor Is-y-coed together with lands having a total area of 70a 31p. The £12 annual income derived from this bequest was to be paid to the vicar for preaching a sermon every Sunday afternoon and the remainder to the master of the school. Later bequests in 1753 reveal that he left a total of £400 in money, the interest of which was to be used not only to supplement the schoolmaster's salary and enable him to train apprentices but also to teach *gratis* six nominated poor children. These children were "to have blew coates and caps, shoes and stockings provided yearly and given to them at Christmas by the Vicar of Ruabon". The children should wear the clothes at all times or forfeit them. The children were to be dismissed at the age of 12 and others elected to the room in their place. Even as late as the 19th century, the school was referred to as the 'Blue Coat School'.

During this period other citizens of the parish also endowed the school, namely Ellis Lloyd of Penylan, Edward Lloyd of Plas Madoc, Randle Jones of Penybryn, Griffith Hughes of Pentre Issa, John Probert, Church Lawton and Richard Davies (vicar of Ruabon 1706–46).

Ironically, whereas these endowments contributed greatly to the continuation and welfare of the school, their specific provisions made it difficult for the school to continue as a 'classical' grammar school.

The essential characteristic of such a school at that time was not the teaching of English but the teaching of the classical languages of antiquity, Latin and Greek. Initially, in such a school, the younger boys conversed with one another in English but the older boys were obliged to speak Latin or Greek at all times. In Wales, these schools were indifferent and even hostile to the Welsh language and Welsh was not allowed to be spoken in them. At Ruabon, the provisions of the endowments meant that the school housed a grammar school and a public elementary school in the same building.

The provision in Robinson's will for the education and clothing of the six boys was repealed in 1872 and Vicar Robinson's prizes were instituted in its place. These prizes, given for religious knowledge, were in the form of books presented to boys at the National Schools of Ruabon, Rhosymedre, Rhosllannerchrugog and Penycae.

Education continued in the 18th century under various schoolmasters. Thomas Evans, Ludimagister, was there for a short time, followed by the Rev. David Prydderch (*c*1711–*c*1759). The numbers of pupils dwindled in this period from about 40 in 1738 to about 20 in 1753. Two graduate curates were there between 1759 and 1786 before the appointment of Rev. Robert Saunders, A.B. who was master from 1786 to 1824. During his tenure of office the number of scholars increased to 60.

Mr. George Bagley, former mathematics master at Shrewsbury School and headmaster at Hawarden School (1818–24), was appointed headmaster at Ruabon in 1824 and in 1825 he built, at his own expense, a kitchen and brewhouse adjoining the school, with two rooms over them, the total cost of which was £200. The building was thus able to accommodate 81 boys.

In 1837, following a summary of the income of the school, the Report of the Charity stated that: "… for this the master considers himself liable to teach 24 boys reading, writing and accounts gratis including six boys clothed (under Robinson's will) appointed by the Vicar and 12 who are placed in the school by the church wardens and apprenticed as reported. He is also bound, if required, to instruct the boys of the parish gratuitously in the Latin tongue".

Education continued successfully under Mr. Bagley for a number of years. But these were times of political unrest in Wales following the Rebecca Riots and when William Williams, M.P. for a Coventry area, a native of Llanpumsaint and a successful London businessman, proposed a motion in the House of Commons on 10th March, 1846 that an investigation be made into the state of education in Wales, the government succumbed to the pressure. A Commission of Inquiry was formed to carry out the survey. It was led by James Kay Shuttleworth, the first secretary of the Privy Council's Education Committee.

Unfortunately, the three young men nominated by the committee to supervise the survey were unsuitable for the task. They had no experience of teaching underpriviledged children, were completely ignorant of the Welsh language and were thoroughly out of sympathy with Welsh Nonconformity. Their chief assistants were, in the main, totally incompetent. Their religious bias was evident as their chief witnesses were landlords, magistrates and industrialists but the evidence of Nonconformists was seldom used. Poor questioning of the children led to the misinterpretation of their answers.

Their report, published in 1847, did admit that the only schools that existed in every part of Wales were Sunday schools and that, although they criticised the narrowness of the curriculum, they noted that these schools had nurtured generation after generation of scholars who were literate in the Welsh language and who could use the language to discuss abstract ideas.

The report however, showed the scorn with which they treated the Welsh language, their hatred of Nonconformity and, as a result, the deficiencies of the educational system in Wales were greatly exaggerated. It concluded with reports of sexual improprieties and mis-representations concerning the moral and intellectual conduct of the Welsh people. The London press reports blazoned the latter on their front pages, blackening the image of Wales, arousing the anger of Welsh patriots and caused a storm of fury throughout Wales. The Blue Books of the report were everywhere denounced as *Brad y Llyfrau Gleision* (the Treachery of the Blue Books).

In the report, Ruabon school was said to be in a dreadful condition. It stated that: "The glass of the windows was broken and the room neglected and filthy in the extreme. The lumber and dirt appears to have been accumulating for several months and except for some tattered books without covers, there was no vestige of the school which was said to have been once held there." No attendance registers of scholars had been kept for years. Mr. Bagley, who had apparently been in poor health for some time, blamed the situation on the fact he had had no help in the form of curates for years, that no one had visited the school for some time and that the dwindling numbers of scholars was due to the opening of new National Schools at Rhosymedre and Rhosllannerchrugog.

The report, allowing for its inaccuracies, did however focus the attention of the people of Wales on the dreadful state of education at that time and inspired people to advocate change.

A new National School was opened in Ruabon in 1847 but nothing was done about the Grammar School until 1853. It was then that the school was reconstituted. Since its formation, the trustees of the school had been the Bishop of St. Asaph and the Chief Justice of Chester and his associate justices. In 1853, not without protest, this was changed. The Bishop of St. Asaph, together with four new members, Sir Watkin Williams Wynn, the Rural Dean of Wrexham, Hon. Lloyd Kenyon and the Vicar of Ruabon became the new trustees. In December 1853 Mr. Bagley, under pressure, was forced to resign and granted a pension.

It was not until 1855 that Alfred Lee Taylor, the son of a Rochdale solicitor and educated at Corpus Christi College, Cambridge, was appointed headmaster, a post he filled until 1903. The new trustees were dissatisfied with the state of the building and were anxious to raise the standard of education provided now that there were National Schools in the area. The schoolhouse had stood in the corner of the churchyard at the top of Ysgoldy Hill since 1618. In 1858 Sir Watkin Williams Wynn proposed that, "… whereas in consideration of the old schoolhouse and garden and the Cinders Farm (then let at £88 per annum) Sir Watkin would transfer to the school a new house and 3a or 24p of land and a tithe rent charge of £127. 10s.". The school soon moved to this new site near Offa's Dyke.

The celebrated Edwardian novelist, Frank Harris, was a boarder at the school in the 1860s and describes some of his experiences in his book *My Life and Loves*. He mentions being taught Latin, Greek, mathematics, (including trignometry and calculus) and enjoying the facilities provided by the well stocked library. He details the visit of a Cambridge professor to present a sixth former with a scholarship of £80 a year to the university. He was also involved in extra-curricular activities —performing in a play by Plautus (in Latin) and describes the pleasure he had in playing Shylock in *The Merchant of Venice*. Cricket was also played and Frank Harris represented the school as a bowler in the 1st XI.

During this same period R. B. Bagnall Wild was also a scholar and eventually head boy at the school. He gained a scholarship to Caius College, Cambridge where he was senior open scholar and rowed in the college boat. In 1868 he took his degree as a Wrangler, was called to the Bar by the Inner Temple in 1870 and went on to practice on the Northern Circuit and Liverpool Sessions.

A School's Inquiry Commission in 1864 reported the the school had 24 day scholars, who paid for being taught certain subjects, and 26 boarders. Half yearly examinations were held and the scholars were promoted as a result of these. Books were given as prizes once a year. Corporal punishment was not used. The report finally praised the headmaster for his work.

In 1872, following a visit by J. L. Hammond, one of the assistants of the Endowed School Commission, a scheme for the management of Ruabon Grammar School was drawn up and approved by the Secretary of the Board of Education. Apart from changes to the governing body of the school the scheme approved fees paid by middle class board and day scholars but stated that poor boys be admitted by scholarships awarded by competitive examination. The curriculum followed should be — history, writing, geography, arithmetic, drawing and elements of algebra and geometry, vocal music, mensuration and land surveying, natural science, English grammar, composition and literature, Latin and Greek and provision should be made for the teaching of French or German.

Following an inspection of the school a Departmental Committee set up to inquire into higher education in Wales and Monmouthshire reported in 1881 that "the accomodation is hardly adequate for the number now in attendance and there are no classrooms. New buildings however, are regarded as an urgent necessity". There were 65 day scholars and 8 boarders there at the time. It was not until 1889 that the recommendations of the Aberdare Committee were implemented in the Welsh Intermediate Act. Following a scheme for Denbighshire presented in 1894, which included Ruabon Grammar School in its proposals, this was incorporated into the national pattern when the Central Welsh Board for Intermediate Education was instituted.

Finally, in June 1896, the new buildings were officially opened. The *Wrexham Advertizer* reported as follows: "An interesting event in connection with the Welsh Intermediate Education Act took place in Ruabon on Friday, when the new Ruabon County School was opened by Mr. Edmund Peel, J.P.. The buildings are the first ones erected under the act and Ruabon parish has reason to be proud of its new school. It is built on the foundations of the Grammar School which was founded as far back as 1632 but it is to be known in future as the Ruabon County Grammar School, although the inscription over the entrance hall is 'Ruabon Grammar School'. The school buildings consist of a schoolroom 40ft. by 20, a classroom 25ft. by 20, a science demonstration room 24ft. by 20, and a chemistry and physics laboratory and workshop 30ft by 20. The rooms are airy and well ventilated; the sides have glazed dados 4 ft. 6in. high while they have Gothic ceilings with pitchpine curved panels and ornamental tracery in the centres. The fittings, desks, blackboards etc. are of the very best. The entance hall is a very fine one. The lavatory is very roomy and the w.c's. are fitted with Adam's automatic flushing apparatus. The floor of the lavatory is laid with tasselated tiles with neat borders. The science demonstration room is fitted with blinds so that it can be converted into a dark room for the purpose of optical demonstrations. The room is provided with a demonstrator's table and fume closet and one of Professor Strood and Rendall's fine optical lanterns. In the workshop there are two working benches with accommodation for twelve students. Provision has been made so that thirty six pupils may take practical chemistry and physics. The motto of the school, *Absque Labore Nihil* is placed over the fireplace in the schoolroom. The buildings were designed by Mr. Denny of Llangollen and were built by Messrs Jenkins and Jones of Johnstown and reflect great credit upon them, Mr. Rees Evans, contractor's manager having superintended their erection. The headmaster, the Rev. A. L.Taylor, M.A. has had charge of the school for the last forty years and his associates are Mr. D. J. Bowen, B.Sc. (Victoria), Mr. T. H. Pritchard and Mr. J. T. Hughes. Mr. Wilfred (*sic*) Jones, R.A.M. is the music master. As it will be seen from the desciptions of the buildings prominence is given to science. It should be mentioned that there is a good recreation ground near the school."

An extraordinary meeting of the Governors of the school took place in August 1903 and was recorded in a press report of the time.

"Alderman E. Hooson (Chairman) said that, having accepted the resignation of the Assistant Master, Mr. F. Jones, he felt that when advertising for a successor the Governors should have one who could teach Welsh, as Ruabon was a Welsh parish. He proposed that course should be taken as the Central Welsh Board examiners laid great stress on Welsh having a place in the school curriculum. The ability to teach Welsh was an essential qualification. — (Hear, hear)."

The proposal was met with much approval but the vicar of Ruabon, the Rev. J. B. Lewis, could see no sense in it. He believed that the teaching of Welsh was entirely useless and that the language had no literary value whatsoever. Alderman C. Jones, in supporting the proposal, expressed his surprise at the strong remarks made by the vicar and the manner in which he had catechized the chairman. He was even more surprised that while Germans and Frenchmen had taken so much interest in Celtic literature, here was a Welshman disparaging his own language. After a prolonged discussion the proposal was carried.

Many years later two heads of the Welsh department brought great honour to the school. Dr. Geraint Bowen won the chair at the 1946 National Eisteddfod at Aberpennar and was Archdruid from 1978–81. Mr. Bryan Martin Davies was Crown Bard at National Eisteddfods held at Rhydaman in 1970 and Bangor in 1971.

The Rev. A. L. Taylor, the schools longest serving headmaster, died in September 1903. He had served the school faithfully for 48 years and had tranformed the school. He had served under three different sets of governors, had seen radical changes in the education of the scholars and had finally seen new buildings and furniture provided for their use.

Following the death of his old headmaster, Mr. J. R. Roberts, M.A. became the first Nonconformist to be appointed headmaster at Ruabon. He was one of the first scholars at Bangor College and, prior to his appointment in 1904, had been an assistant master at Harrogate College since 1896. His father, the Rev. Thomas Roberts, was a minister at Bethel Chapel, Ponciau and his cousin, I. D. Hooson (another old boy of the school) was to become one of the most renowned poets in the Welsh language. Another famous Welsh poet, R. Williams Parry, pays tribute to J. R. Roberts in an 'englyn', a special form of Welsh verse:

> *Un oedd a'i farn yn ddi-feth — i gynnal*
> *Gwahaniaeth ym mhopeth*
> *Difodwr, cosbwr casbeth*
> *Noddwr mwyn pob addfwyn beth.*

During a speech day at the school in December 1904, Mr. Roberts stated that he had presented eleven candidates for C.W.B. examinations that year, six seniors and five juniors, and that of these ten passed, gaining seventeen marks of distinction. Two scholarships had also been won — one to Liverpool University and one to Aberdeen University.

Mr. E. S. Price also began his duties as a master at Ruabon on the day of the funeral of the Rev. A. L. Taylor and became well known in educational circles for his pioneering work and publications in geography. It was probably under his influence that, when an extra timber-framed hut was added to the school and erected just prior to the Great War (1914–18) the main part of it became the geography room, the remainder, a store-room and staff room.

Mr. J. R. Roberts was appointed headmaster at Cardiff High School in 1917, a post he held until his retirement in 1934. Following his departure, the Rev. D. J. Bowen, M.Sc. acted as headmaster at Ruabon for the following three years. During this time another timber-framed hutment was acquired to provide four extra classrooms.

The Rev. D. J. Bowen had been on the staff of the school for many years prior to his appointment as headmaster on 27th March, 1920. He was of the firm opinion that the school had been founded in 1575 by the then vicar of Ruabon, Dr. David Powel, who acted as its first headmaster until his death in 1598. Dr. Powel assisted Bishop William Morgan in translating the Bible into Welsh and also wrote a history of Wales. Mr. Bowen may have mistakenly thought that the curates whose names appear in the first Ruabon Parish Registers acted as schoolmasters. Consequently, during his tenure of office, the school badge was changed so as to include not only the date 1575 and the crest of the Prince of Wales (granted following a visit of Prince Charles to the school in 1623) but also Dr. David Powel's arms — a blue lion rampant, white ground, ermine. Below the shield was the school motto

ABSQUE LABORE NIHIL

At the annual Prize Distribution Day at the boys' school in April, 1925 the headmaster reported that there were 211 pupils at the school and that during the year ten boys had moved on to a university. The annual school Eisteddfod, which had been a private gathering until 1919, was now open to the public and held in May. Mr. Daniel H. Jones, M.A. of Johnstown was the guiding force behind the Eisteddfod. At the 1925 Eisteddfod, Arwel Hughes, the renowned conductor and composer, won the prize for the best original melody. In 1950, he was appointed resident conductor of the Welsh Symphony Orchestra and in 1965 became Head of Music at the B.B.C. in Cardiff, a post he held until his retirement in 1971.

Plans for new science buildings at the boys' school had been drawn up by the county architect as far back as 1908. The buildings were not erected until 1928. They were officially opened by Principal Emrys Evans of Bangor on November 13th of that year. Apart from providing a chemistry laboratory and prep. room, physics laboratory and prep. room, they also included a storeroom and three classrooms. The contractor for the building works was W. E. Samuel of Wrexham. The cost of the building was £8,100 and a further £750 was spent on laboratory furniture. The timber framed hut which provided a geography room, store room and staff room, together with another hut providing four classrooms, were retained. These buildings completely surrounded what became known as the 'quad', with covered areas on the sides so that pupils could shelter in inclement weather.

The Rev. D. J. Bowen retired in 1938 and became rector of Whitewell. He had been on the staff of the school for a total of 48 years and had seen great improvements to the facilities provided for the pupils. There were now 270 boys at the school and fourteen members of staff.

Mr. J. T. Jones, M.A. a former pupil at the school and further educated at U.C.N.W. Bangor, was appointed headmaster in 1938. Before his appointment as assistant master at Ruabon in 1921 he had taught Welsh and Latin at Denbigh Grammar School.

New extensions to the boys'school were officially opened on July 23rd 1941 by W. J. Williams Esq., M.A. Chief Inspector of Schools in Wales. The school had been remodelled so as to include extra classrooms, a library, prefects room, assembly hall, geography room, art room, gymnasium, medical room, changing room with bath and showers, headmaster's room, staff room, cloakrooms, latrines, ablution block, and a kitchen attached to the existing dining room. The total cost of the extensions was £21,250.

Mr. J. T. Jones M.A. retired in 1953. The school had received an inspection prior to his retirement and at the School Speech Day held in April he was obliged to report on its findings. He did this in his own inimitable manner, showing his complete mastery of the art of oration. The guest speaker, Dr. Edwin A. Owen, professor of physics at U.C.N.W. Bangor, stated that he had never heard such an excellent report as that given by Mr. Jones. Referring to the report published following the Ministry of Education Inspection Dr. Owen added, "… it is one which should make the school exceedingly proud of its headmaster and staff".

Mr. R. R. Pearse of Pentre Bychan, who had been senior mathematics master at Ruabon since 1922, succeeded Mr. Jones. He had graduated B.Sc. with first class honours in Pure and Applied Mathematics at the University of London, heading the college list and had served as the senior mathematics master at the High School, South Shields for a short time before his appointment to Ruabon. A member of the Welsh Joint Education Committee since 1952 (the only assistant master from a grammar school in Wales to be so), he had been appointed Deputy Head of the school in 1947.

In July 1964, Mr. R. R. Pearse retired and at his official presentation Mr. R. E. Davies (Deputy Headmaster), who presided over the ceremony, said that "Mr. Pearse had got right into the life of the school since he first arrived in 1922 and had all along instilled into his pupils a sense of goodness, seriousness and purpose in life". Mr. H. Parry, in presenting the retirement present, said that Mr. Pearse's work had been characterized with zeal and competence and that he had preserved the highest traditions of the school, intellectually, morally and culturally. In his dealing with the staff, he was full of understanding, patience and courtesy.

Mr. R. E. Davies acted as headmaster of the school during the autumn term of 1964 and in January 1965 Mr. Eifion Ellis, B.A. (who had previously been Deputy Headmaster at Fishguard Comprehensive School), was appointed to the headship.

In 1967 the Ruabon Boys Grammar School and the Ruabon Girls Grammar School amalgamated and became a single comprehensive school under the combined headships of Mr. E. Ellis and Miss Ethel Wood. This was the end of grammar school education at the two Ruabon schools near Offa's Dyke.

1. School Badge

This impressive tiled school badge hangs, even today, on the east wall of the Crush Hall. The school badge was probably changed by the Rev. D. J. Bowen in 1927 so as to include the date 1575. Below the Prince of Wales' Feathers crest at the top, the coat of arms is made up of: 1st quarter: red dragon rampant, 2nd and 3rd quarters: lions of England and the fleur de lys of France and 4th quarter: the arms of Dr. David Powel, a blue lion rampant, white ground, ermine. The school blazer remained blue in colour until the 1930s even though games kits were green and red.

2. The rear view of the Original Grammar School, Ruabon, taken in 1925 from the church yard showing, on the left, the schoolroom with the kitchen, brewhouse etc. added by Mr. Bagley in 1825 and, on the extreme right, part of the hearse shed.

3. The Rev. Alfred Lee Taylor
Headmaster 1855–1903.

4. Mr. J. R. Roberts, M.A.
Headmaster 1904–17.

5. Ruabon School Football Team at the turn of the century,

6. Ruabon School Cricket XI early this century.

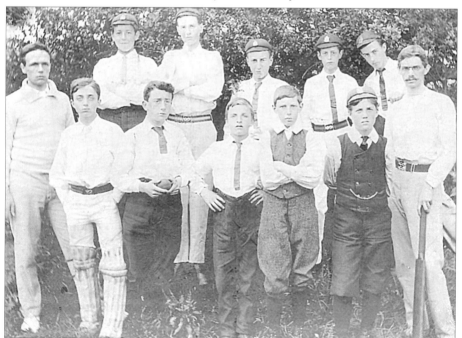

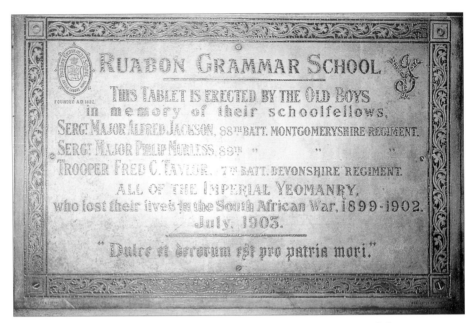

RUABON GRAMMAR SCHOOL

THIS TABLET IS ERECTED BY THE OLD BOYS
in memory of their schoolfellows,
SERGT MAJOR ALFRED JACKSON, 88TH BATT. MONTGOMERYSHIRE REGIMENT.
SERGT MAJOR PHILIP MORLESS, 88TH " " "
TROOPER FRED C. TAYLOR, 7TH BATT. DEVONSHIRE REGIMENT.
ALL OF THE IMPERIAL YEOMANRY,
who lost their lives in the South African War, 1899-1902.
July, 1903.

"Dulce et decorum est pro patria mori."

7. Boer War Memorial
This brass tablet is on the west wall of the dining room.

At every Remembrance Day service, held each year in the assembly hall, the names of old students who had lost their lives in previous wars were read out, and a bell tolled outside the door after each name was called. The old school badge can be seen in the top left corner of the tablet and below it the words "Founded in 1632".

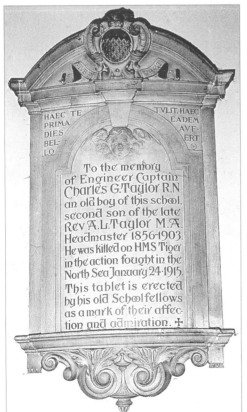

HAEC TE PRIMA DIES BELLO

TVLIT HAEC EADEM AVFERT

To the memory of Engineer Captain Charles G. Taylor R.N an old boy of this school, second son of the late Rev A. L. Taylor M.A. Headmaster 1856-1903. He was killed on HMS Tiger in the action fought in the North Sea January 24 1915. This tablet is erected by his old Schoolfellows as a mark of their affection and admiration. ✝

8. The Memorial to Engineer Captain Charles G. Taylor
This plaque, in memory of the son of the Rev. A. L. Taylor (Headmaster 1855–1903) remains on the east wall of the old dining room.

9. Ruabon Grammar School A.F.C., 1918-19
Back: Ben Davies, W. T. Griffiths, Mr. D. B. Jones (Sportsmaster), Eric
Bowen (Captain). *Middle:* Arthur Jones, Gwilym R. Hughes (Secretary),
Trevor Davies. *Front:* Tecwyn Bates, J. Albert Jones, Idris Bowyer, Harold
Richardson, Moses Williams.

10. Ruabon Grammar School A.F.C., 1920 - 21

11. A Form or House Photograph, *c.*1922
Mr. J. Scott Archer and the Rev. D .J. Bowen are seated at the centre.
Osian Edwards is on Mr. Archer's right and Arwel Hughes stands in the
back row, 2nd from the left.

12. Ruabon Grammar School C.C., 1925
Mr. E. P. Jones, Mr. R. E. Davies and Mr. J. Scot Archer stand at the rear
and the Rev. D. J. Bowen and Mr. R. R. Pearse are seated at the front.

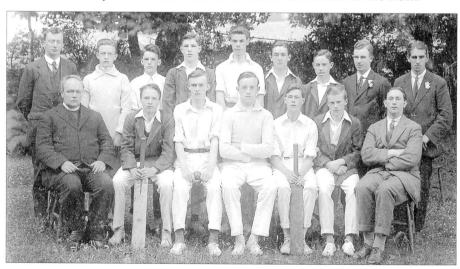

13. Ruabon Boys' Grammar School Staff, 1925
Back: Mr. E. P. Jones, Mr. T. Parry, Mr. R. R. Pearse, Mr. R. E. Davies and Mr. J. S. Archer. *Front:* Mr. M. Ware, Mr. D. B. Jones, Rev. D. J. Bowen, Mr. E. S. Price and Mr. J. T. Jones.

14. Ruabon Grammar School A.F.C., 1927–28
Back: Mr. R. R. Pearse, E. Williams, I. Evans, W. T. Jones, J. B. Jarvis, Mr. E. P. Jones. *Middle:* Rev. D. J. Bowen, E. Williams, H. Bowen, C. Hewitt, -?-, M. Roberts, Mr. J. Scot Archer. *Front:* O. Edwards, -?-, -?-, J. Brown.

15. Opening of the New Science Buildings, 1928
Principal D. Emrys Evans, M.A., B.Litt. sits in the centre with Alderman
Christmas Jones, J.P. on his right. The Rev. D. J. Bowen, M.Sc. together with
Mrs. Deborah Jones, Mrs. Gwladys Jones and Mrs. R. A. Jones sit on his left.
Miss Mary Jones, M.A. stands behind the Rev. Bowen. Mr. & Mrs. Ifor
Bowen stand in the back row together with members of staff.

16. Ruabon Grammar School C.C., 1928
W. H. Brown, A. W. Brown, T. J. Hughes, E. G. Parry, W. T. Jones,
B. Jones, J. S. Bowen, Mr. R R. Pearse. Rev. D. J. Bowen, L. H. Davies,
J. O. Edwards, J. H. J. Bowen (Capt.), J. A. E. Davies, J. E. Brown,
Mr. H. E. Parry.

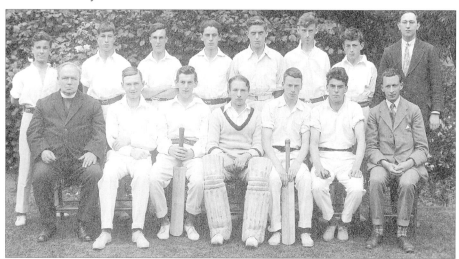

17. Ruabon Grammar School A.F.C., 1928–29
Played 13: Won 11: Lost 2. Goals for 78: Goals against 28.
Back: Mr. E. P. Jones, H. W. Jones, E. G. Parry, W.H. Brown, H. Shaw,
W. L. Jones, Mr. R. R. Pearse. *Front:* T. Francis, R. E. Thomas, T. J. Hughes,
Rev. D. J. Bowen, G. Roberts (Capt.), J. B. Jarvis, J. M. Charles.

Ruabon Boys' Grammar School 1927–33 — Johnie Morgan

From the first day of our admission to the school, we were made conscious of the fact that we were now pupils of a GRAMMAR SCHOOL - a school with great traditions and founded in 1575 (it was claimed). We were impressed and happy to be told that Wednesday would be a half day, but not too thrilled when told that we were expected to attend school on Saturday mornings. Furthermore, we were to be at school each day at 8.50 a.m. promptly; otherwise we would be placed on the detention list and detained on Wednesday afternoons. To ensure punctuality each boy had a numbered tally which, on arrival at school, he would place on the appropriate hook on a board which was removed at 8.50 a.m. The school atmosphere and activities bore the effects of the 1914-1918 World War and the miners' strikes of 1921 and 1926. Classes were still held in Army Huts and Physical Education was based on army drill. We were ordered to stand in lines;- ' Shortest to the left, tallest to the right ' —'Form -fours' —' Quick march '— which we did for almost an hour, with pieces of wood carved in the shape of rifles held on our shoulders.

Fortunately, our admission in 1927 coincided with a period of many changes and improvements. New buildings housing Chemistry and

Physics Laboratories and spaceous classrooms had been opened. Four new,younger teachers were appointed to replace retired, promoted and, in one case, deceased, members of staff. One of the new teachers had been educated at a well known rugby playing school, Llandovery College and also at Oxford. It transpired that some members of Staff believed that the status of the school would be greatly enhanced Ruabon if became known as a rugby-playing school. So, in 1930, the first Ruabon Grammar School Rugby Team was formed, much to the disappointment of a number of senior boys who had contributed to historic victories on the soccer field and some of whom distinguished themselves at College and University levels.

There was a language gulf between the the mostly Welsh speakers of Rhos, Ponciau, Pen-y-cae and Johnstown and the non-Welsh speakers of Cefn, Ruabon,Acrefair and Rhosymedre, which was reflected in the choice of subjects studied - with very notable exceptions. The choice of the Arts by the Rhos pupils was indicated by the preponderance of teachers and preachers from the village. The Cefn pupils favoured the Sciences, no doubt influenced by career prospects provided by the rapid development of Monsanto Chemical works. The boys from Rhos who went on to study at Universities or Teacher Training Colleges found that the standard of achievement attained at Ruabon Grammar School compared favourably with that of other schools throughout Wales but those of us who had chosen to study Welsh as part of our courses found it very difficult to obtain parity with students from other schools who had studied Welsh Grammar, Literature and Poetry. At Ruabon, Welsh speakers and non-Welsh speakers were offered only 'Easy Welsh', showing a distinct lack of respect and status for the Welsh Language in those days. I suppose we should have been warned.On the school's impressive badge were the words: ABSQUE LABORE NIHIL. *Mewn geiriau eraill: HEB LAFUR —
DIM.*

18. Ruabon Grammar School Annual Camp, Tenby 1930
J. B. Jarvis, H. W. Jones,
T. Phillips, K. Francis,
J. Charles, and Ivor Jones.

19. Ruabon Grammar School R.F.C. 1931–32
Back: Mr. E. P. Jones, H. Hanmer, S. -?-, D. Roberts, F. Gittins, A. Turner,
H.W. Jones, Lloyd Massey, T. Phillips, Mr. H. Parry. *Middle:* Mr. R. Pearse,
B. Charles, B. Latham, D. Owen (Capt.), Rev. D. J .Bowen, T. Francis,
T. Jones, J. E. Jones, Mr. H. W. Jones. *Front:* E. W. Furmstone, J. Morgan,
M. Edwards, H. O. Hughes.

20. Annual Prize Distribution, 1935
Standing: J. B. Davies, R. E. Davies, W. D. Jones, E. P. Jones, R. R. Pearse,
E. S. Price, Rev. R. Crossdale (Penylan), E. Jones, H. Parry, J. T. Jones, T. Parry,
R. I. Davies, and H. W. Jones. *Seated:* S. Davies, Rev. D. J. Bowen, Lord Bishop
of St. Asaph, Rev. Dr. W. Davies, Dr. C. Davies. The photograph was taken at
the front entance of the Board School.

Ruabon Boys' Grammar School — Glyn Edwards.

There cannot be many of us left who remember being taught French, Welsh and Latin in those ex-army huts, the fourth of which housed the Form VI and completed one side of the 'Quad'. The only attributes of this hut were the hinged windows which opened downwards to reveal interesting glimpses of the girls over the boundary fence, providing , of course, one stood on the desks.

We must have been a very fit crowd of younsters, walking as we did from Rhos, Ponciau, Cefn and Acrefair to school six days a week. The reason for the Saturday attendance was shrouded in mystery but may have been due to the limited availability of the part time art master. The most popular route from Rhos to school was through Pant Farm, down to the obnoxious fumes of the Brandie Sewage Works, then up the long climb to the ridge of the Gardden and finally down to Offa's Dyke. If the weather was inclement we resorted to the road way, through Pant, Copperas, skirting Plas Bennion and 'Top Field'. Very rarely, depending on the staff and the timing, we would be offered a lift in the Guard's Van of the brick train from Rhos to Plas Bennion level crossing. Then sometimes, in the Summer term, we would dawdle home through 'Rocky Woods' occasionally cooling our feet in the mountain stream. We must have saved the Education Authority thousands of pounds. Why did we not think of claiming a shoe leather allowance?

To enhance our fitness even further we endured P. T. under the control of Tom. Parry, our Welsh Master, whose forceful instructions were quite specific: 'When I shout WAN, you jump up, and when I shout TWO you come down.' Then we would struggle up to Top Field for our sports activities under the supervision of Hywel Wyn Jones, our Chemistry Master and a Cambridge 'Blue' at both soccer and rugger.

This brings me to a very controversial episode when soccer in the school was replaced by rugby. Protests brought the responce that too many students were giving up acedemic studies to become professional footballers — I can remember only two . The result was that many students played their football for local teams.

The highlight of the Ruabon day was the school dinner and it was wonderful to see Dai (the school caretaker) and Mrs. Davies carrying the steaming trays of bangers and mash to the Assembly Hall where the dinner tables and trestles were erected. Here the great priority was to elect the table waiter most swift of foot to avail his colleagues of generous second helpings.

It was the practice for staff and pupils to present annually the Shakespearean play chosen for the C.W.B. examination that year, with J. Scott Archer, the English Master, as producer. In my first year, by some mischance, I found myself in the cast of *The Tempest* and became known for the next two or three years as Ariel.

Mr. R. E. Davies forsook his Physics laboratory on occasion to give us woodwork instruction in a quaint little room near the main gate. All I remember is planing purposeless bits of wood and spending an inordinate amount of time counting the tools at the end of the period to ensure that no one had hidden a chisel in the lining of his blazer.

It was quite a happy school, with accredited smoking areas and the occasional flogging drama. But perhaps the happiest recollection we have is of being young and healthy, enjoying sport , bangers and mash. Ah, well!

21. *The Merchant of Venice,* **1934**
Standing: Noel Jones, Don Jones, Eurof Jones, John Arther Thomas, Wilfred Lloyd, –?–, Basil Morton. *Seated:* Meredith Edwards, Mr. Hubert Parry, Miss Summerton, Miss Lousi Wittington, Miss Marian Hughes, Mr. J. Scott Archer and Jim Ashton. *Front:* Geoffrey Williams.
The play was produced by Mr. J. S. Archer who also played Shylock and wrote the incidental music, *Moonlight in Belmont*. Meredith Edwards went on to play at the Liverpool Playhouse and the Old Vic. He appeared in many television programmes and his films included *Run for your Money, The Blue Lamp, The Lavender Hill Mob, The Cruel Sea. The Trials of Oscar Wild* and *The Great St. Trinian's Train Robbery.*

29

Ysgol Ramadegol, Rhiwabon.

Ruabon Grammar School.

Founded 1575 A.D.   Endowed 1632 A.D.

Annual Prize Distribution

Wednesday, January 30th, 1935, at 3-0 p.m.

Speaker:

*The Right Reverend The Lord Bishop
of St. Asaph.*

The Prizes will be distributed by The Lord Bishop.

Chairman:

The Reverend Dr. Wynn Davies, O.B.E.

23. Ruabon Grammar School R. F. C. 1935–36

Played 14, Won 12, Drawn 1. Points for 78 against 28.
Back: H. K. Rees, T. Davies, W. E. Chidlaw, E. Jones, D. O. Jones, J. C. Ashton,
D. Ll. Newton. *Centre:* M. Blackwell. J. B. Morton, J. A. Thomas,
Mr. R. R. Pearse, Rev. D. J. Bowen, A. A. Jones (Capt.), J. R. Powell,
D. H. Edwards. *Front:* G. Charles, G. Williams.

24. *The Widow of Ephesus*, 1936.
Tom Charles, Hubert Parry, Don Newton (the corpse), Emma Bellis, Wyn
Cunnah and Vera Thomas. The Old Pupils Association entered this play in
the Wrexham Drama Festival. The unpredicable often happens in live theatre
and when the play was performed at the George Edwards' Hall, Cefn, the
soldier's spear somehow became entangled in his uniform. In trying to free
the spear the soldier managed to knock the corpse off the rostrum on to the
front of the stage. The curtains were drawn immediately leaving the corpse in
full view of the audience. Like a true professional, Don Weston raised
himself slowly to his feet, rubbed himself down as if it was part of the act,
and walked majestically off the stage to tumultuous applause.

25. Ruabon Grammar School C.C., 1936.
Back: H. Smith, G. H. Jones, N. Jones, T. davies, D. O. Jones, P. H. Pritchard,
T. K. Jones. *Front:* K. Williams, J. A. Thomas, M. Blackwell, Mr. R. R. Pearse,
Rev. D. J. Bowen, A. A. Jones (Capt.), E. G. Robertson, G. S. Watkin.

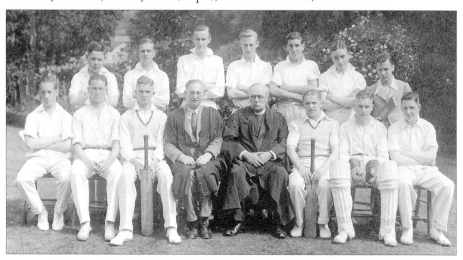

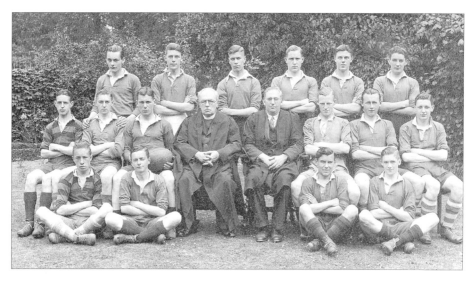

26. Ruabon Grammar School R.F.C., 1936–37
Back: C. T. Hughes, R. Jones, G. Thomas, G. Griffiths, C. Jones (a), C. Jones (c),
Middle: E. Rogers, C. V. Hughes, G. Williams (Capt.), Rev. D. J. Bowen, Mr. R.
R. Pearse, T. Davies. *Front:* R. S. Hamlet, G. S. Watkin, K. Williams,
J. F. Sellers, P. Roberts, E. B. Jones.

27. Ruabon Grammar School C.C., 1937
Back: C. K. Mitchell, C. V. Hughes, G. Thomas, R. S. Hamlet, V. Wright,
K. Williams, H. Smith. *Middle:* J. F. Sellers, P. H. Pritchard, T. Davies (Capt.),
Rev. D. J. Bowen, Mr. R. R. Pearse, N. Jones, G. Williams, G. S. Watkin.
Front: E. Evans, E. Rogers

28. Footpath

This footpath lying west of Offa's Dyke, well worn by hundreds of students from Cefn, Acrefair and Rhosymedre, was also used by senior pupils during lesson breaks when satisfying their craving for nicotine. A clearing on top of this Dyke provided an ideal place for physics students to focus the telescopes of their spectrometers on the pinacle of Wyatt's Obelisk in Wynnstay Park, this being considered as infinity. Here also, after school hours, senior pupils came to settle any unresolved disputes —a scene of much bloodshed and strife.

29. Crush Hall

The inscription above the main entrance to the crush hall of 1895 states again that the school was founded in 1575 and must have been made when the Rev. D. G. Bowen was headmaster, probably in 1927.

30. *One Hundred Years Old,* **1938**
Front stage area: Emrys Charles, Vera Roberts, Emma Bellis, Olwen Mears and
Johnnie Morgan. This Spanish play, which was performed by the Old Pupils
at the Miners' Institute in Rhos, was produced by Miss Emma Bellis.

31. Ruabon Grammar School R.F.C., 1938–39
Back: D. Grimley, T. P. Jones, P. G. Lloyd, D. Jones, Mr. R. R. Pearse, E. V. Jones,
E. Latham, J. R. Jones (Capt.), Mr. R. E. Davies, J. A. Pritchard.
Middle: T. G. Brown, G. Smith, E. B. Jones, Mr. J. T. Jones, G. Thomas,
W. V. Evans, J. Cooper. *Front:* F. Roberts, R. C. Blundell.

32. Cricket 1st XI, 1939
Back: Mr. R. E. Davies, T. P. Jones, J. L. Morris, E. G. Jones, Mr. R. R. Pearse,
J. G. Ellis. *Middle:* R. Nicholas, C. Giller, G. Thomas (Captain), Mr. J. T. Jones,
E. B. Jones, A. J. Bennett, H. W. Charles. *Front:* D. Grimley, E. R. Jones.

33. Ruabon Grammar School R.F.C., 1939–40
Back: Ken Jones, G. W. Jones, A. Nicholas, C. O. Evans, D. Shellard, S. Roberts,
A. Valentine, E. Latham, H. Charles, Mr. R. E. Davies. *Middle:* J. R. Jones,
D. Jones, E. V. Jones (Captain), Mr. J. T. Jones, J. Cooper, F. Roberts,
W. V. E. Evans. *Front:* G. V. Roberts, T. P. Jones, R. C, Blundell, E. Ethelston.

34. Ruabon v Grove Park , 1939

This photograph was taken in front of the cricket pavilion on top field. The Ruabon boys are in their usual red and green striped shirts and are in the middle of the photograph. From the back: R. Blundell, J. Cooper, G. Smith, Eric Latham, S. Roberts and D. Jones, J. R. Jones, J. T. E. Brown, E. V. Jones, P. Roberts, B. Jones, G. Thomas, F. Roberts, W. V. E. Evans, P. Lloyd.

35. Cricket 1st XI, 1940

Back: Mr. R. E. Davies, L. Evans, T. C. Jones, T. Ellis, M. Davies, A. Edwards, D. Griffiths. *Front:* T. Jones. C. Hughes, T. P. Jones, H. Charles, Mr. J. T. Jones, J. Cooper, E. V. Jones, F. Roberts.

36. Rugby 1st XV, 1940–41
Back: Mr. R. E. Davies, T. A. Lloyd, T. Ellis, D. Shellard, B. Hannaby, S. Hill,
W. N. Rees *Middle:* R. Bowen, C. O. Evans, A. Nicholas, F. Roberts (Capt.),
Mr. J. T. Jones, E. Latham, M. Davies, C. D. Griffiths, J. R. Jones.
Front: H. Duchett, C. W. Jones, N. Pritchard, E. A. Jones.

37. Cricket 1st XI, 1941
Back: R. T. Ellis, T. C. Jones, J. R. Jones, N. Nicholas, B. Hannaby, D. T. Jones,
M. Davies, Mr. R. E. Davies. *Front:* H. Roberts, R. Bowen, F. Roberts (Capt.),
Mr. J. T. Jones, T. Ellis, D. Griffiths, S. Hill.

38. Rugby 1st XV, 1941–42
Back: Mr. R. E. Davies, L. Morris, E. W. Evans., D. Powell, T. Ellis, E. Jones, J. B. Roberts, T. C. Jones, N. Rees. *Front:* B. Hannaby, A. Nicholas, J. R. Jones, F. Roberts (Capt.), Mr. J. T. Jones, D. Shellard, R. Bowen, V. G. Bowen, V. P. Jones.

39. Cricket 1st XI, 1942
Back: B. Edwards, J. R. Jones, B. Hannaby, J. B. Roberts, N. Nicholas, T. Dutton. *Front:* G. Charles, H. Roberts, F. Roberts (Capt.), Mr. J. T. Jones, Mr. R. E. Davies, T. Ellis, R. Bowen, T. C. Jones

40. Dining Room
The ceiling with its ornamental tracery dominated the dining room, where, after grace was said in English, Welsh, French or Latin depending on the duty master, monitors were dispatched quickly to the kitchen hatches to fetch the food and plates and enable the head of each table, with the help of his deputy, to distribute the food, fairly or unfairly, to their juniors. The tables were normally set with one end against the wall and the head of table sitting on the other end.

41. Combined Rugby and Soccer Teams, 1942–43
Back: R, Bates, G. Charles, S. Hill, J. B. Roberts, B. Hannaby, H. O. Evans,
T. C. Jones, D. Evans. *Middle:* H. Roberts, G. Howard, R. Bowen (Capt.
Rugby), Mr. R. E. Davies, Mr. J. T. Jones, G. Bowen (Capt. Soccer), V. P. Jones,
Cyril Davies. *Front:* D. Powell, J. G. Williams

42. Cricket 1st XI, 1943
Back: G. S. Jones, G. Charles, J. A. R. Bates, D. B. V. Powell, J. B. Roberts,
V. G. Bowen, C. Jones, E. B. Jones. *Front:* W. B. Hannaby, D. F. Evans,
R. Bowen (Capt.), Mr. R. E. Davies, Mr. J. T. Jones, V. P. Jones, H. V. Roberts,
R. S. Hill.

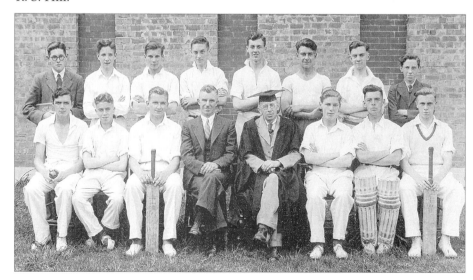

43. Football 1st XI, 1943–44
Back: E. B. Jones, J. A. R. Bates, G. O. Phillips, J. B. Roberts, G. Charles,
E. T. Williams, D. Davies, Mr. R. E. Davies. *Middle:* D. B. V. Powell,
D. F. Evans, T. C. Jones (Capt.), Mr. J. T. Jones, J. G. Williams, C. B. Dodd,
D. Speake. *Front:* J. R. Williams, L. B. Broadbent.

44. Cricket 1st XI, 1944
Back: S. Matthews, J. A. R. Bates, G. O. Phillips, J. B. Roberts, E. T. Williams,
 J. A. C. Williams, Mr. R. E. Davies. *Middle:* D. Davies, J. G. Williams,
T. C. Jones (Capt.), Mr. J. T. Jones, G. Charles, D. F. Evans, D. Powell.
Front: P. D. Potts, E. B. Jones.

45. The Main Entrance

To an 11 year old boy entering the 'quad' via this impressive main entrance was an awe inspiring experience and once there watching open mouthed as a tall, slightly greying, elegant master wearing a tattered mainly black gown, useful for cleaning blackboards, strode purposefully across the 'quad' to the school bell which he tolled with metronomical precision.

46. The 'Quad'

This view from the 'quad' shows part of the extensions built in 1895, with the door leading into the Crush Hall at the centre. The gable end of the dining room is on the left, and the lecture theatre on the right. Both of these photographs were taken in 1999.

47. Football 1st XI, 1944–45

Back: Mr. J. B. Davies, J. A. R. Bates, K. V. Davies, D. Davies, J. C. Wilson, G. Morris, J. G. Connah, Mr. R. E. Davies. *Middle:* W. G. Jones, J. D. Griffiths, G. Charles (Capt.), Mr. J. T. Jones, D. F. Evans, G. O. Phillips, J. T. Darlington. *Front:* J. R. Williams, G. Griffiths

48. Cricket 1st XI, 1945

Back: G. S. Pemberton, D. Jones, J. A. R. Bates, H. W. Edwards, J. C. Wilson, G. Morris, D. Davies, Mr. R. E. Davies. *Front:* S. Matthews, P. D. Potts, G. Charles (Capt.), Mr. J. T. Jones, D. F. Evans, G. O. Phillips, J. A. C. Williams.

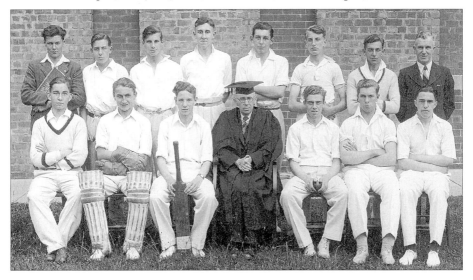

Ysgol Rhiwabon a'r Awen — Gwynne Williams.

Diachos yw Rhydychen,
Am fod Art ym Meifod wen!

Dene brofiad un o Gywyddwyr Powys erstalwm! Wel, dwn i ddim beth am hynny, ond dwy neu dair blynedd yn ol roeddwn i'n gyrru drwy fryniau'r Costwolds a'm bryd ar ben y daith yn Rhydychen. Yn sydyn mi weles i arwydd yn y gwrych yn cyhoeddi'n ddigon swil i'r byd a'r betws bod y ffordd ar y chwith yn arwain i Adlestrop. Ac ar unwaith roeddwn i'n ol yn y Rhydychen ragorach honno — Ysgol Ramadeg y Bechgyn Rhiwabon hanner canrif ynghynt!

Bore oer o Ionawr a ninnau, fechgyn heglog, esgyrniog dosbarth un o'r Rhos a'r Ponciau, Rhiwabon a'r Cefn Mawr, yn gwrando'n geg-agored ar Ma Pearse yn cyflwyno telyneg Edward Thomas i ni ac yn ein hannog, nage, yn ein siarsio ar berygl ein heinioes, i'w dysgu ar ein cof erbyn y bore wedyn. O leiaf, roeddwn i'n gwrando'n geg-agored. Ac er na wyddwn i bryd hynny, ble yn y byd yr oedd swyddi Caerloyw a Rhydychen, heb son am Adlestrop, wrth i holl adar cerdd y ddwy sir honno agor eu pigau yn niwl y prynhawn, y syrthies i am y tro cyntaf, o dan gyfaredd barddoniaeth Saesneg.

Cof sal sydd gen i am rai pethau ond mi alla i gofio'n glir y tro cyntaf yr es i i'r ysgol honno i eistedd yr hen sgolarship bondigrybwyll 'ne. Roedd pymtheg ohonon ni o Ysgol y Rhos wedi mentro ar y daith bws geiniog a dimai i ben-draw'r-byd ac yn eistedd yn nerfus o dan olwg barcutaidd rhywun wynebgoch, cecrus, ceg-gam a heb wybod beth ar wyneb y ddaear i'w ddisgwyl. Yn siwr ddigon, doedd yr un ohonon ni'n disgwyl y dyn bach sbatiog, crys gwlanog a sgubodd i mewn trwy'r drws y bu o'n anelu agoriad at berfedd twll ei glo o'r ochr arall i'r cwod.

Yn ddiweddarach, wedi mynd adre'r pnawn ne yr eglurodd nhad pwy ydoedd y J. T. hwn. Yn ddiweddararch o lawer y sylweddoles arwyddocad gweithred fidogaidd y 'goriad. Fe fu o'n hyrddio drysau ar agor led y pen i fechgyn Dyffryn Maelor drwy'i oes.

Mi rydw i hyd yn oed yn cofio beth a wisgai o y bore hwnnw. Ond peidiwch, da chi, a meddwl bod hynny'n gamp eliffantaidd. Na chwaith bod gen i ryw ffetish wyrgam am ddillad pobl. Y gwir amdani, wisgodd o ddim byd gwahanol yn ystod yr holl amser y bum i yn Rhiwabon. Er, i fod yn deg, efallai y dylwn nodi mai dim ond am bedair blynedd olaf ei deyrnasiad y cefes i'r fraint o eistedd wrth sbatiau'r Gamaliel hwn. Ie, yr hen sbatiau diddorol! Ond mwy cyfareddol oedd ei fantell. Bu hon unwaith yn ddu, eithr roedd blynyddoedd o inc, sialc, grefi lympiog y cantin, ac yn ol mabinogi'r dosbarthiadau isaf, gwaed bechgyn drwg - rhai'r Cefn, wrth gwrs, —wedi ei britho.

Eithr nid lliw ei fantell ond ei llun a'ch trawai chi gyntaf. Haf neu aeaf, hindda neu ddrycin, roedd hi wastad chwe modfedd yn is ar yr ochr dde nag ar y chwith. A doedd hi ddim yn syth ar yr ochr honno o bell ffordd chwaith. Mewn gwraig byddai'r ffasiwn yn ddiddorol. Diddorol ond anweddus. Un pesychiad go iawn, ac fe deimlech y datguddid y cyfan. Un pesychiad? Fe'i gweles o'n cyflawni ystumiau bygythiol y byddai trywsus byr a chylch focsio yn fwy addas ar eu cyfer. Mewn gorchestion cosbyddol cyhyrog a wnai i Bedwyr ei hun wrido fe'i gweles, do, ac fe'i teimles, pan

> Chwifiodd ei fraich ufudd fry,
> A'i ffon drosto drithro a drodd,
> Onid oedd fel darn o dan,
> Y din ar ol y driniaeth!

Ond mi alla i roi fy llaw ar fy nghalon, a dweud na symudodd y fantell 'ne yr un blewin. Rioed! Fwy na'r blewin hwnw oedd ganddo fo ar draws ei gorun y dyddiau hynny. Un oedden nhw, y fo a'i fantell.

Ac ar ol y pibydd brith hwn yr heidien ni yn y gwersi Sgrythur yn dyrfa fodlon, ddedwydd i Balesteina — oedd y dyddie braf hynny, rywle tu draw i Gyfelie i fechgyn y Rhos — ac i Lanfair-y-llin yn y gwersi Cymraeg. Ac ar un o'r teithiau difyr hynny, yng nghwmni J. T., y llithrodd rhyfeddod prin yr awen Gymraeg o'm blaen am y tro cyntaf erioed. Fe ddiflannodd llwynog R. Williams dros y grib, mae'n wir, ond mae dwy sefydlog fflam ei lygaid yn dal i syllu arnaf uwchlaw ei untroed oediog.

Fel y gwnaethon nhw y bore hwnnw yng nghwmni J. T. yn Ysgol Ramadeg Y Bechgyn Rhiwabon hanner canrif bron yn ol.

49. Football 1st XI, 1945–46

Back: J. Thomas, J. D. Griffiths, B. Jones, P. D. Potts, K. V. Davies, W. Matthews (?), Mr. R. E. Davies. *Middle:* J. A. G. Connah, G. O. Phillips, D. F. Evans (Captain), Mr. J. T. Jones, G. Morris, J. T. Darlington, G. Griffiths. *Front:* S. Roberts, D. W. Gilpin.

50. Cricket 1st XI, 1946
Back: G. Pemberton, T. E. Jones, E. Ellis, G. Williams, W. Matthews, J. Thomas, Mr. R. E. Davies. *Front:* J. C. Wilson, P. D. Potts, D. F. Evans (Capt.), Mr. J. T. Jones, D. Jones, G. Morris, G. O. Phillips.

51. Football 1st XI, 1946–47
Back: A. B. Ellis, T. P. Jones, J. Baraclough, H. Davies, S. Evans, N. Williams, Mr. R. E. Davies. *Front:* J. Connah, L. Tunnah, G. Griffiths (Capt.), Mr. J. T. Jones, D. W. Gilpin, J. T. Davies, J. Griffiths.

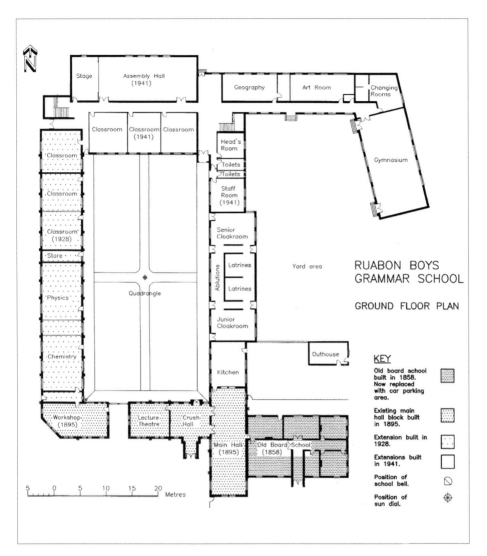

The plan shows a ground floor plan with the following labels:

N

Stage | Assembly Hall (1941)

Geography | Art Room | Changing Rooms

Classroom | Classroom (1941) | Classroom

Head's Room

Toilets
Toilets

Staff Room (1941)

Gymnasium

Classroom

Classroom

Classroom (1928)

Store

Physics

Chemistry

Quadrangle

Senior Cloakroom

Ablutions | Latrines

Latrines

Junior Cloakroom

Yard area

RUABON BOYS GRAMMAR SCHOOL

GROUND FLOOR PLAN

Outhouse

Kitchen

KEY

Old board school built in 1858. Now replaced with car parking area.

Existing main hall block built in 1895.

Extension built in 1928.

Extensions built in 1941.

Position of school bell.

Position of sun dial.

Workshop (1895) | Lecture Theatre | Crush Hall

Main Hall (1895) | Old Board School (1858)

5 0 5 10 15 20 Metres

52. Plan of the Boys' School
Showing the developement of the school from the old Board School of 1858 to the extensions built in 1941.

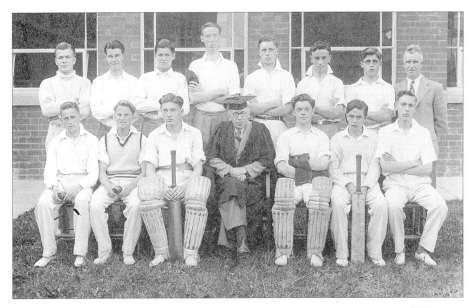

53. Cricket 1st XI, 1948

Back: P. Britton, J. Connah, T. P. Jones, J. Baraclough. J. B. Jones, J. Hughes, J. Griffiths, Mr. R. E. Davies. *Front:* E. Ellis, L. Tunnah, D. W. Gilpin (Capt.), Mr. J. T. Jones, G. Griffiths, G. Parry, T. E. Jones.

54. Football 1st XI, 1948–49

Back: R. J. Jones, P. Williams, G. Humphreys, G. Hughes, J. Bowen, Steele, L. Green, T. Rawlings, G. P. Jones, H. Hannaby, Mr. R. E. Davies.
Middle: Mr. J. T. Jones, N. C. Williams, J. T. Davies, J. Baraclough (Capt.), J. Griffiths, D. Evans, N. Williams, Mr. J. B. Jarvis. *Front;* B. Charlton, B. Price.

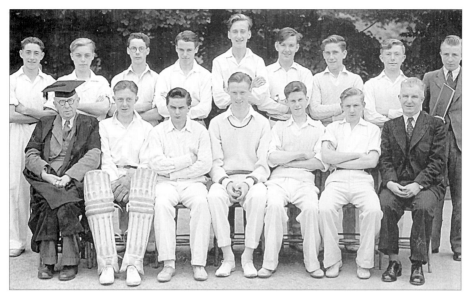

55. Cricket 1st XI, 1949
Back: M. Ward, E. Roberts, S. M. Roberts, P. Williams, T. Rawlings, J. Bowen,
B. T. Hughes, G. Hughes, I. G. Davies. *Front:* Mr. J. T. Jones, L. Green,
G. Parry, J. Baraclough (Capt.), B. Price, R. J. Jones, Mr. R. E. Davies.

56. Staff Cricket Team, 1949
Back: J. B. Jarvis, H. Parry, G. John. R. Hamilton, E. H. Clements, G. Bowen,
R. R. Pearce. *Seated:* J. Groves, A. E. Pillinger, R. E. Davies, V. Davies,
E. Bowyer. *Front:* W. J. Bowyer.

57. Football 1st XI, 1949–50
Denbighshire Grammar Schools League Champions.
Back: Mr. E. Bowyer, G. Valentine, P. Williams, R. J. Jones, J. Bowen, L. Green,
T. Rawlings, R. E. Watkin, N. Griffiths, –?–, N. Thrift. *Front:* Mr. J. T. Jones,
Hannaby, E. Dodd, G. P. Jones (Capt.), D. E. Evans, B. Griffiths, G. Hughes,
Mr. J. B. Jarvis.

58. Cricket 1st XI, 1950
Back: Mr. V. Davies, G. Valentine, J. Bowen, J. O. Jones, T. Rawlings,
P. Mullally, P. Williams, B. Hughes ?, Mr. J. Groves. *Front:* Mr. J. T. Jones,
D. E. Evans, E. Roberts, S. M. Roberts, B. T. Hughes (Capt.), R. J. Jones,
L. Green, I. G. Davies, P. Kilfoyle.

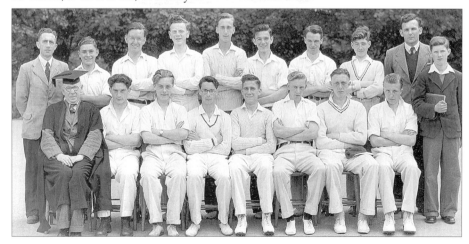

59. *Julius Caesar*, 1950
Standing at the back are John Fisher and Peter Crewe and below them stand
Peter Hilton Jones, and Derek Oldfield. Front of stage stand: Alun Williams,
Bryn Lawrence, Derwyn Morris Jones, Peter Williams, Clive Roberts. Ken
Jones, Gareth P. Hughes, Elwyn Dodd, John Williams, Brian Hayes, Glyn
Parry Jones, Elwyn Jones, Alan Griffiths and David Williams.
Sets and properties were designed and constructed at school under the
direction of Mr. J. R. Jones and Mr. Maelor Griffiths. Mr. R. Hamilton was in
charge of lighting and the play produced by Mr. Gwilym V. John.

60. VI Form Geography Class on the Gardden, 1950
Back: S. M. Roberts, R. M. Jones, B. Lawrence, B. T. Hughes,
J. O. Jones. *Front:* G. P. Jones, E. Roberts, R. E. Watkin.

61. Football 1st XI, 1950–51
Back: Mr. E. Bowyer, C. Roberts, G. V. Davies, R. J. Jones, L. Green, E. Dodd, C. Owen, H. Hannaby. *Front:* Mr. J. T. Jones, G. Valentine, C. Jones, G. P. Jones (Capt.), T. Davies, S. Darlington, Mr. J. B. Jarvis.

62. *Adventure Story* **(Terence Rattigan), 1951**
Back: George Digby Lloyd, Colin Whittall, Tudor Davies, Peter Hilton Jones, Alan Griffiths, Gareth P. Hughes, Elwyn Dodd, J. B. Davies, Derwyn Morris Jones, Courtney Owen, Keith Pritchard, Clive Griffiths, Derek Oldfield, Gwynne Thomas, Peter Kilfoyle and Peris Pritchard Jones.
Front stage: Malcolm Taylor, Kinross Almond, John Fisher, Brian Hayes, Dafydd Prosser and Basil Dodd. The effects were managed by Ieuan G. Davies and Leslie Green and the play was produced by Mr. Gwilym V. John.

63. Cricket 1st X1, 1951
Back: A. James, G. P. Jones, G. R. Jones, G. D. Lloyd, D. Gittins, I. G. Davies, O. B. Roberts, H. P. Kilfoyle. *Front:* Mr. J. T. Jones, G. Valentine, L. Green, R. J. Jones (Capt.), J. O. Jones, P. B. Mullaly, Mr. V. Davies.

64. Athletics Team, 1951.
Back: Mr. R. Hamilton, E. Williams, R. Franks, K. Roberts, K. Pritchard, R. Dodd, A. James, C. Hayes, C. Owen, Mr. J. Groves. *Middle:* Mr. J. T. Jones, E. Dodd, S. Darlington, G. A. Williams, G. P. Jones, G. B. Jones, J. Johnson, C. Jones, Mr. E. O. Bowyer. *Front:* Richard Everitt, R. Jones, B. Dodd, Keith Hannaby, N. Whomsley, N. Ellis.

65. Football 1st XI, 1951–52

Back: Mr. E. Bowyer, A. James, C. Whittall, P. B. Mullaly, L. Green, R. Dodd, G. Thomas. C. Owen, C. Roberts. *Front:* Mr. J. T. Jones, S. Darlington, H. P. Kilfoyle, E. Dodd (Capt.), T. Davies, G. Valentine, Mr. J. B. Jarvis.

66. Cricket 1st XI, 1952

Back: A. James, J. Fisher, G. R. Jones, B. Woolrich, D. Roberts, O. B. Roberts, H. P. Kilfoyle, G. Valentine, Mr. V. Davies. *Front:* Mr. J. T. Jones, D. Gittins, G. D, Lloyd, L. Green (Capt.), I. G. Davies, P. B. Mullaly, K. Morris.

67. Athletics Team, 1952

Back: Mr. R. Hamilton,, N. Ellis, B. Williams, H. Richards, G. P. Hughes, P. Mullally, K. Pritchard, B. Hayes, P. B. Jones, C. Roberts, T. Bates, D. Oldfield, Mr. J. Groves. *Middle:* Mr. J. T. Jones, S. Darlington, R. Everitt, G. B. Jones, R. Dodd, C. Owen, J. Johnson, Mr. E. O. Bowyer. *Front:* G. O. Kilfoil, B. Dodd, Huw –?–, J. A. Jones, N. Whomsley, T. Rowlands, D. Evans, R. Blythin.

68. Ruabon Boys Grammar School Staff, c1953.

Back: A. Lloyd, J. R. Jones, J. B. Jarvis, J. Groves, T. Owens, M. Griffiths, M. Morgan, E. O. Bowyer, G. Bowen. *Front:* Clements, R. E. Davies, Mrs. Pearse, J. T. Jones, R. R. Pearse, H. Parry, G. V. John.

69. Cardiff Trip, 1953

Back: V. Pritchard, E. Richards, N. Samuels, D. Jones, M. Roberts,
D. Evans, M. Potts, D. Jones, D. Roberts, G. Griffiths.
Front: G. Thomas, L. Phillips, D. Davies, Roberts, G. Tinsley,
T. Pemberton, G. Jones, G. Davies, J. Blackwell, J. Roberts, –?–.

70. Football 1st XI, 1952–53

Back: Mr. E. O. Bowyer, C. Roberts, D. Gittins, G. R. Jones, B. Edwards,
R. Dodd, G. P. Hughes, C. Hayes, Mr. J. Groves. *Front:* Mr. J. T. Jones,
D. Hughes, D. Williams, G. Valentine (Capt.), C. Owen, Mr. J. B. Jarvis.

71. The Quad

The four lawns of the 'quad', were each kept in immaculate condition by members of the four houses Madoc, Cynwrig, Rhuddallt and Wynnstay, but today look rather neglected. The sun dial (*Tempus Fugit*) has been removed and the glass covered shelters surrounding the 'quad' have been vandalised and are in need of repair.

72. The School Yard

The school yard was where we bought pop (Tom Charles's, if I remember correctly—T.C.P.) from Dai the caretaker, played marbles, conkers and 'sigo', and where some interested pupils watched open mouthed as the VIth Form girls passed by to the old Board School and where others gauped at the antics of the girls in the gymnasium. On sunny days Mr. E. S. Price would place his slides to dry on the steps leading to his room.

73. Cricket 1st XI, 1953

Back: Mr. J. Groves, B. Edwards, D. Gittins, G. R. Jones, L. V. Roberts, N. Ellis, R. Jones, K. Almond, Mr. Tom Owens. *Front:* Mr. J. T. Jones, M. Taylor, B. Roberts, G. Valentine, J. Fisher, Mr. E. O. Bowyer.

74. Athletics Team, 1953

Back: Mr. J. Groves, D. Hughes, D. Evans, T. Rowlands, B. Dodd, C. Roberts, G. P. Hughes, R. Jones, J. A. Jones. *Front:* Mr. J. T. Jones, C. Owen, C. Hayes, R. Dodd, J. Johnson, R. Blythin, Mr. E. O. Bowyer.

75. Football 1st XI, 1953–54
Back: Mr. G. Charles, J. Fisher, C. Roberts, R. Powell, R. Jones, B. Edwards,
D. Gittins, N. Ellis, D. Hughes, K. Almond, Mr. J. Groves. *Front:* Mr. R. R.
Pearse, G. R. Jones, G. P. Hughes, C. Owen (Capt.), A. James, G. D. Jones, Mr.
E. O. Bowyer.

76. Athletics Team, 1954
Back: A. James, C. Roberts, T. Rowlands, J. Hughes, F. Simon, G. P. Hughes,
B. Edwards, J. A. Jones, G. Pritchard, E. Cookson, K. Davies, Mr. J. Groves.
Front: Mr. R. R. Pearse, D. Evans, R. Jones, D. Gittins, C. Owen, N. Ellis,
G. E. Kilfoil, Mr. E. O. Bowyer.

77. Cricket 1st XI, 1954

Back: Mr. S. Matthews, R. Powell, D. Evans, K. Almond, G. P. Hughes,
L. V. Roberts, B. Roberts, B. Edwards, A. Jones, Mr. E. O. Bowyer.
Front: Mr. R. R. Pearse, A. James, D. Gittins, G. R. Jones, R. Jones, J. Fisher,
N. Ellis, Mr. J. Groves.

78. Football 1st XI, 1954–55

Back: G. D. Jones, R. Jones, F. Simon, C. Roberts, B. Edwards, G. Jones,
T. Rowlands, D. Gittins, *Front:* Mr. J. Groves, N. Ellis, J. B. Jones,
Mr. R. R. Pearse, C. Owen (Capt.), D. Williams, Mr. E. O. Bowyer.

Security in the Age of Enlightenment — Geoffrey E. Kilfoil

Despite sounding like a chapter heading in Southgate's history text book for Form V, it may be considered a summing-up of the two central solid pillars of what an institution such as the Ruabon Grammar School meant to perhaps more than just one ten year old pupil whose career there began on 13th September 1949 and ended in mid 1957.

All Ruabon Grammar School pupils had spent one notable 'Scholarship Day' exploring through and around porches of proportions undreamt of, using lavatories which unbelievably were indoors and roofed, trying washbasins in a row of seeming infinity, lining up in a glass-roofed bottle-green wrought iron-posted verandah alongside a sun-dialled and lawned inner quadrangle in pupil numbers never before experienced. Then waiting (between the English and arithmetic examinations) to go in to dinner in a hall which then appeared huge in dimension but which, on the first day as an actual pupil, was overtaken by the Olympian proportioned staged Assembly Hall and later in that first week by the the first gym they had ever seen.

To discover oneself to be a part occupier of such an institution and buildings was the start of a new experience which, by an unconscious alchemy, had turned full circle by the time of leaving so that the institution had become so much part of one's personality that one felt a proprietor's stake in the school.

Security and enlightenment first derived from the organization of the year's new entrants, alphabetically, into Form I —up to about halfway through the Joneses into IA and from there down to the Williamses into IB. Membership of one of the four school 'Houses' (Cynwrig —yellow; and the lesser other three, Madoc —red, Rhuddallt —blue and Wynnstay —green) accorded to each of the fifty-odd new entrants, ensured that there was a meeting-point which transcended the rough and ready first term's division and maintained a stratum of unity throughout their school careers. This unity was strengthened by each member of staff being attached to one or other of the 'Houses' and by the mighty striving for points in the annual school inter-house eisteddfod, football matches or on sport's day.

Thus one became a member of a group of 50 plus pupils, composed of lads who had never met before, from villages and areas distant and foreign to one's native village; some indeed were totally unknown by both name and location — Tai Nant? Rhosymadoc? However, travelling through the next half-dozen years in the almost daily company of at least the core of those fellow pupils, provided that confidence required to step outside of one's *'milltir sgwar'*, secure in the expectation that one might rely on friendship with contemporaries to provide a safe point of reference and an ally 'abroad'. The background to this process owed much to the manageable and intimate size of the school population (probably less than 300) and based on an intake from a circle of individually characteristic villages, all within a compass of a couple of miles of each other and of the school.

On leaving, one left behind each staff member's idiosyncrasy of character, his or her individual trait — even of physical motion, each mode of speech and phrase peculiar to an individual, each especial expression of countenance, each foible — as a pupil perceived them to be. The 'Staff' had its own stability deriving from its apparent unchanging composition. It did change, but it seemed so rarely; there always seemed to be a substantial 'rolling' core of continuity not only in numbers of staff but also in the essentially unchanging ethos of the staff which infused the corporate life within the school with a solidity and security which one took for granted at the time but which can be fully appreciated in retrospect.

That continuity of security was enhanced by the fact that members of staff lived in the same villages as their pupils, so providing a mutuality of existence. There would be the history master (Hubert E. Parry, grand-nephew of Dr. Joseph Parry) who might offer a lift in his grey A35 when a pupil had cut it fine to complete his run to school from Acrefair over the Dyke from Tir y Fron by 9 a.m. There would be the geography master (J. Brynmor Jarvis) and, after his appointment in 1953 as Richard R. Pearse's successor as mathematics master, Gwilym Charles, either or both of whom might well be standing but a few yards from a pupil on the Racecourse kop. There was the new geography master, Selwyn Matthews, who was appointed after the 'interregnum' of his relative Mary Saunders (the Girls' Grammar School geography mistress) who kept the geography department on course after J. B. Jarvis' appointment to the headship of Basingwerk School. Selwyn persuaded a number of us from the Acrefair/Cefn area to take up hockey and join him in the Monsanto team. That this conveniently provided us with the imprimatur to form a R.G.S. boys' team which could engage in the legitimate close contact sport with the R.G.S. girls' hockey team was a purely fortuitous pupil-led extension (rather than staff inspired) of the enlightenment process.

In 1949, in Form 1B room, there was a large piece of newly acquired radio equipment by means of which the geography master, J. B. Jarvis, introduced us to a "music appreciation period" in which a 10 year old boy entered the unknown world of symphonic and other orchestral music so that he cannot now hear the 'Swan' cello solo from St. Saen's *Carnival of the Animals* without vividly seeing and hearing that 50 year old experience. Similarly, any of Dvorak's *Slavonic Dances* brings back memories of the use of one of those dances as incidental music to the school's dramatic production of *A Midsummer Night's Dream* —plus the still vivid sweet smell and greasy feel of the make-up applied to one's face, hands and wrists by the staff 'production and management' team in the dressing room which took over the school library pro tem.

Hubert Parry's fiefdom was not simply Form VA classroom (which was also his history teaching room) but extended to an enlightened despotism in the library, a room which occupied almost the whole of the side of the upper corridor opposite the opened areas of wall through which one could look into the the assembly hall below. Here 'H.P.' instituted a truly Byzantine complexity of rules governing the use of the library which included the removal of and lining up of footware before entry, special seating positions and catagories of approved reading matter depending entirely upon his subjective assessment of the prospective reader's capability.

Mr. J. B. Jarvis was the master denizen of the geography room and the 'Dark Room'. It was also his Form IVA classroom and his command "Close desks!", issued in a voice scarcely above the level of soft breathing, was to be obeyed with desk closures that were equally as quiet; any miscreant's failure to do so was met with an expression of such eye-narrowed, pained disappointment that it would be but a feckless fool who would be unaware of the master's disapproval.

A particular feature of the 1950s period was the variable modes of transport adopted by or indulged in by staff. The Headmaster rarely resumed his seat on his erstwhile trusty motor-cycle, preferring the geography master's motor car. Mr. and Mrs. Pearse shared the French master's motor car. The woodwork master's 3-wheeler motor car was 'handcrafted' from materials and in a local 'factory', both quite unknown to the rest of the British motor industry. His arrival each morning in the main 'quad' was greeted by somewhat ironic —or perhaps sympathetic— applause and his homeward journey's preliminary motions were achieved only by the use of pupil power across the 'quad' until by some lucky chance a form of quasi-motorised independant motion spluttered forth.

There was the classics master's small, black, Morris Series 'E' family saloon, driven with grim faced determination and at a pace as deliberate as its owner's pedestrian movement. If he was not beaten by the school Crosville single-decker to the corner round the parish church lych-gate, hearts would sink knowing that the bus would have to patiently follow the motor car from the church to school, whilst those pupils on bicycles or even on foot overtook both bus and car.

The few experiences touched upon in the foregoing paragraphs are each non-pareil examples of the synthesis of staff and pupils which forged the personality of more than one boy who was privileged to have passed through Ruabon Grammar School.

79. 1st Prize Winners at the 1955 Eisteddfod.

Back: C Thomas, G. E. Jones, J. B. Jones, M. Davies, G. E. Kilfoil, G. Gittins, A. Wulmer, L. V. Roberts, B. S. Edwards, J. Fisher, D. Gittins, J. Nelson, R. Taylor, A. Davies, E. Williams, K. Broadbent, D. S. Jones. *2nd:* D. Smith, P. Pemberton, C. Roberts, A. Richards, G. Williams, M. Strong, D. Williams, D. Jones, R. Williams, D. Jones, G. Richards, K. Almond, G. P. Jones, B. Ll. Hughes, N. Owen, A. Clayton, G. Parry, P. Wood, B. Williams, D. Meredith. *Front:* D. Jones, J. James, –?–, D. Furmstone, D. Williams, B. Morris, J. W. Roberts, D. Jones, A. Thomas.

64

80. Prefects, 1956
Back: A. Thomas, G. F. Williams, M. Davies, G. Gittins, (?) Coxon,
Front: J. V. Thomas, A. Davies, J. E. Davies, Mr. R. R. Pearse, G. E. Kilfoil,
G. Roberts, J. W. Edwards.

81. Football 1st XI, 1956–57
Back: O. M. Edwards, K. Richards, G. Pritchard, J. A. Jones, R. Towey, J. Pugh,
E. Bellis. *Front:* Mr. R. R. Pearce, T. Pugh, H. Bowyer, P. Hughes (Capt.),
G. Kilfoil, M. Roberts, Mr. E. O. Bowyer.

82. Form I, 1956

Back: M. Bishop, M. Buckley, M. Charles, G. Corfield, P. Davies, V. Dodd,
R. Dyer, E. Edwards, M. Edwards, I. Ellis, C. Evans. *Middle:* J. N. Evans,
J. S. Evans, K. W. Evans, C. Green, B. Griffiths, C. Griffiths, G. Griffiths,
J. V. Griffiths, A. Griffiths, B. Hughes. *Front:* G. Jenkins, A. P. Jones,
B. G. Jones, C. Jones, G. W. Jones, G. Jones, J. W. Jones, W. J. Jones, W. Lloyd.

83. Form I, 1956

Back: E. W. Methren, D. Morris, D. W. Morris, D. J. Morris, R. Morris,
A. Moreton, D. Parrish, A. Phillips, R. Pickering, D. Price, S. Pritchard.
Front: A. Richards, P. Richards, D. Roberts, R. Roberts, D. Roberts,
J. L. Roberts, P. Roberts, S. Roberts, D. Robinson, J. Taylor, D. Thomas.
G. Thomas, R. Thomas, A. Williams, D. Williams, H. Williams, J. E. Williams,
D. Wright, G. Jones.

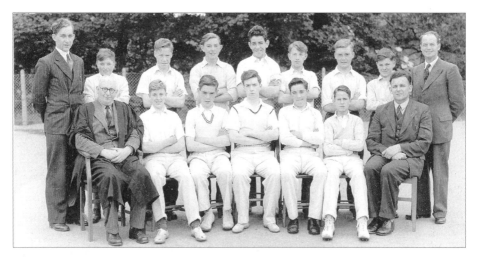

84. Cricket 1st XI, 1956

Back: Mr. S. Matthews, D. S. Jones, V. Pritchard, Elfyn Richards, J. A. Jones,
O. M. Edwards, E. Cookson, N. Bowyer, Mr. E. O. Bowyer.
Front: Mr. R. R. Pearse, N. Whomsley, D. Hughes, G. E. Kilfoil, D. Harris,
B. Hughes, Mr. J. Groves.

85. Football 1st XI, 1957–58

Back: M. Roberts, R. G. Pritchard, D. Jones, T. Bishop, D. Edwards, R. Tovay,
E. Bellis. *Front:* Mr. R. R. Pearse, D. Rowley, T. Pugh, T. Rowlands (Capt.),
O. M. Edwards, K. Richards. Mr. E. O. Bowyer.

86. Athletics Teams, 1959
Back: B. Jones, J. S. Evans, B. Morris, B. Edwards, D. Williams, D. Rowley,
T. Richards, J. Elks, B. Potts, J. H. Griffiths, G. Williams, J. Rowley.
Front: Ll. Jones, G. Northall, R. Edwards, G. Pritchard, I. J. Evans, I. Hughes,
J. Evans, Mr. R. R. Pearce.

87. Cricket 1st XI, 1959
Back: H. Roberts, W. Turner, L. Rawlings, J. Davies, M. Richards, D. Formstone.
Front: Mr. R. R. Pearce, P. Davies, J. W. Roberts, O. M. Edwards (Capt.),
G. Freeman, B. Potts, Mr. S. Matthews. Ruabon G.S. defeated Gresford to win
the cup.

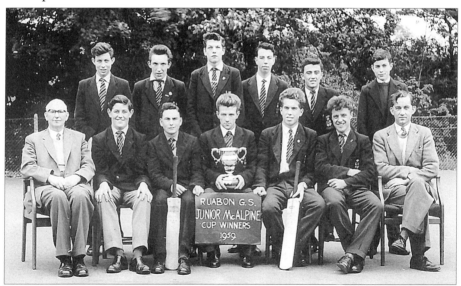

88. The French Trip, Easter 1960

This was the scene early one Easter morning on the platform of Ruabon Station. The French master, Mr. Gordon Banks, had arranged this visit to St. Bonnet-le-Chateau with Mr. Lester V. Roberts, an old pupil of Ruabon who had spent some time teaching at this French school. At the back are: Richard Williams, Mr. Banks, Huw Morris, Gareth Davies, Grevin Jones, Mr. L. Sudworth and John Land. At the front: Merfyn Thomas, Elfed Roberts, Peter Boaz, Stafford Evans, John Barry Edwards and David Griffiths.

89. Form IIA, 1962

Back: E. G. Charles, R. Edwards, M. Field, K. Goodman, P. Ll. Hesketh, D. E. Hughes, R. C. M. Hughes, R. A. Hughes, B. C. Isaac, D. G. Jones. *Middle:* T. M. Jones, W. J. Jones, J. A. Lane, D. Lewis, J. H. Lloyd, J. G. Lloyd, T. M. Mile, S. C. Morris, P. I. Phillips. *Front:* O. M. Powell, J. Read, A. Roberts, D. N. Roberts, J. E. Sheen, J. B. Thelwell, A. Thomas, C. P. Thomas, B. Tunnah.

90. Staff, 1964
Back: G. Hughes, (?) Pritchard, A. Davies, S. Matthews, G. –?–, B. M. Davies.
Middle: K. Goodwin, G. Charles, D. Owen, J. Bradbury, W. Carling,
G. P. Hughes, L. Sudworth. *Front:* M. Griffiths, J. R. Jones, R. E. Davies,
R. R. Pearse, H. Parry, E. O. Bowyer, J. Groves.

91. Football 1st XI, 1964–65
Back: J. McHale, J. Clarke, S. Evans, A. Thomas, D. Taylor, G. Pritchard,
M. Griffiths. *Front:* E. Miles, J. Prydderch, A. Fisher, P. Pritchard, K. Jones.
This team went on to play in the Ivor Tuck Cup semi-final in South Wales
after beating Grove Park 4–2 in the quarter final.

92. The Staffroom, *c*1964
J. R. Jones, J. Bradbury, B. M. Davies, G. Charles and
E. O. Bowyer relax in the small staffroom.

93. Madoc Football Team, 1965
Back: J. McHale, A. Thomas, M. Williams, S. Wright, P. Jones, I. Diggory.
Front: D. Valentine, R. Davies, J. Clarke, E. Miles, T. Jones.

94. Rhuddallt Football Team, 1965

Back: G. Pritchard, I. Jones, P. Pritchard, C. Jones, D. Taylor, W. Williams.
Front: J. Prydderth. M. Griffiths, B. Drake, P. Price, S. Evans. Peter Price went
on to play for Liverpool and Peterborough.

95. Form IA, 1964–65

Back: P. K. Arthur, R. W. Bolton, A. M. Catherall, M. A. Coates, G. D. Corfield,
K. S. Cox, J. A. Cullum, I. T. Darlington. *Middle:* J. R. Davies, K. L. Edwards,
P. S. Evans, J. B. Fowles, R. Francis, E. C. Griffiths, A. Hamer.
Front: D. G. Hughes, J. A. Hussey, J. K. Jarvis, C. Jones, D. W. Jones, G. W. Jones,
P. W. Jones, T. S. Jones.

Bryan Martin Davies 1959–78 June 1999

I was appointed to the post of Assistant Master in the Welsh Department at Ruabon Boys Grammar School in 1959, became Head of the Department when Dr. Geraint Bowen left in 1961 and remained at the school until 1978. These early years of my career, until the school was reorganised into a Comprehensive School in 1967, were some of the happiest and richest of my life and I feel very privileged to have been there at that particular time.

I remember a previous headmaster, Mr. J. T. Jones once saying in one of his eloquent adjudications of the Chair Competition in the School Eisteddfod; 'Nid lle ydy'r Rhos, ond pobl. ' He was a master of rhetoric, but this observation of his could also be applied to the school. It was not merely a place, an unremarkable red brick building situated on the edge of Offa's Dyke, it was a closely integrated society of people; staff and pupils, men and boys, forged sometimes willingly, sometimes precariously, into a community devoted to what was then rather grandly described as the pursuit of learning. At times, this complex structure of relationships was very successful, at times it failed, but there was a joy about it all which is not easily forgotten.

My first impression of the pupils was in my first School Assembly on a sunny September morning in 1959, in a surprisingly impressive school hall. Before me stood an amorphous mass of green blazered boys, standing in neat rows, well turned out, and singing the opening hymn with remarkable confidence, indeed, with a gusto and musicality which I had never before encountered in any school. It had an amazing maturity of harmony about it, which made me realise at once that the glorious musical tradition of this enclave of Welshness on the 'gororau' was not a mythical one. I soon realised however, that these hymn singing paragons of choral excellence were also boys skilled in deception, regularly proficient in roguary, sometimes lazy, sometimes workish, and always keen observers of all human frailities which they so rapidly perceived in their elders. They were to be watched, but they were delightful. I could name many, especially the very good ones and the very naughty ones, but they were all a joyful celebration of the human condition, in all its strengths and weaknesses.

Amongst the staff I remember very distinguished men, some scholarly and dedicated to their profession, some more ironic, and indeed, quite self critical of their own attempts at being successful teachers. We were all very close to each other, keenly aware of our particular beliefs and prejudices. We invariably teased each other, sympathized with each other, goaded each other, and at times comforted each other. The truth is that, in that rather shabby little staff room, I made some of the most enduring friendships of my life.

I have always considered my years at Ruabon Boys' Grammar School as a labour of love. One must always labour to love and that, maybe, is the essential truth of the old school's motto: ABSQUE LABORE NIHIL

96. Form I Alpha, 1964–65
Back: M. W. Lacey, C. D. Lawton, D. A. Lewis, P. Morris, W. M. Owens,
R. Pealing, K. Phillips, P. G. Powell. *Middle:* M. R. Pugh, E. M. Pumford,
M. A. Richards, D. T. Roberts, J. S. Roberts, C. Smith, J. P. Smith, D. Thomas.
Front: R. W. Tipton, J. Tunnah, B. D. Watkins, J. H. Williams, M. Williams,
P. L. Williams, S. Williams.

97. Form VI, 1964–65
Back: K. Munford, W. T. Jones, –?–, I. Diggory, T. Grounds, J. Clutton,
W. Williams. *Middle:* T. M. Williams, B. Price, C. Lloyd, I. A. Jones,
S. Wright, B. Drake, C. Green. *Front:* E. O. Hughes, A. Fisher, G. Owens,
(?) Massey, F. Williams, A. R. Hughes.

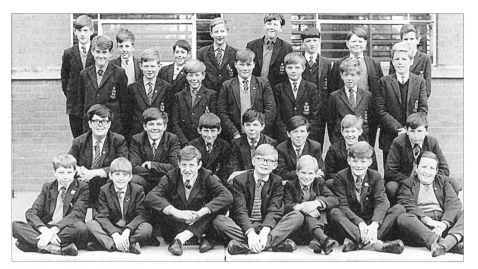

98. Form IIA, 1964–65

Back: J. G. Alexander, R. P. Bellingham, C. W. Blaine, K. Ll. Davies, P. H. Davies, W. A. Davies, S. Duckett, M. Evans. *Second:* D. Griffiths, P. M. Hanmer, D. Hughes, D. M. Humphreys, I. K. James, D. I. Jones, D. St. J. Jones. *Third:* G. C. Jones, G. S. Jones, R. Jones, R. I. P. Jones, A. Lloyd, M. Lloyd, D. V. Nash. A. Owens, D. W. Owens, R. Parry, L. Pemberton, G. P. Phillips, P. Read, G. Roberts, H. J. Roberts, G. K. Talbot, B. T. Williams.

99. A happy group in the 'Quad,' *c*1964

Standing: H. Roberts, F. Evans, J. H. Griffiths, B. Morris, M. Wright, B. Williams, V. Edwards, P. Prydderch, D. Say, B. Puwsey, G. Williams, A. Thomas, J. Evans, H. Williams. *Sitting:* R. Heyward, D. Jones, T. Smith, D. Formstone, R. Crocombe, H. Thomas, V. Williams, (?) Parrish, M. Thomas.

100. Chairing of the Bard, *c*1966

P. Pritchard, P. Evans, D. P. Roberts, V. Williams, Mr. B. M. Davies, D. G. Jones (Chaired Bard), M. Roberts, G. V. Thomas, A. D. Williams, C. C. Jones, J. Button, J. A. Daniel.

101. Form VI, 1966–67

Back: M. Edwards, D. Westbrooke, Philip Arthurs, M. W. Davies, D. Richards, D. A. Williams, Wladyslaw Letocha, J. Roberts. *Second:* H. Moysen, I. V. Roberts, H. Davies, G. V. Thomas, T. C. Evans, P. Griffiths, A. Carless, D. Nicholas. *Third:* D. W. Peters, M. Roberts, V. Williams, C. Jones, R. Williams, J. Lloyd, D. P. Roberts. *Front:* P. Pritchard, G. Pritchard, P. Drake, M. Griffiths, A. A. Thomas, J. C. Jones, C. C. Jones, J. A. Daniel.

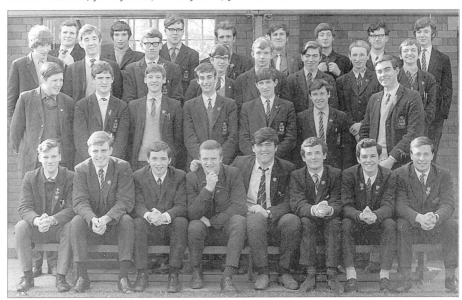

102. Form I Alpha, 1966-67
Back: H. C. Lacey, V. Legge-Thomas, C. A. W. Mills, B. V. Minton, G. W. Parry, A. H. Richert, D. A. Roberts, D. H. Roberts. *Middle:* P. Roberts, P. W. Schleising, J. M. Talbot, G. Thomas, P. V. Thomas, T. Thomas, M. Valentine. *Front:* A. C. Williams, A. Williams, C. Williams, M. F. Williams, R. E. A. WIlliams, T. A. Williams, W. B. Williams, J. A. Wright.

103. School Corridor
This was the loneliest place on earth if you had been sent to see the headmaster and were imagining the dreadful consequences of your misdemeanours.

GAUDEAMUS.

104. The Ruabon Boys Grammar School Song

Guadeamus Igitur, was a student song of the Middle Ages the melody of which was used by Brahms in the concluding part of Op. 80 *Akademische Festouverture* which he wrote in celebration of the honorary doctorate he received from the University of Breslau in 1879.